HOW TO DRAW
FAIRIES

David Antram

BOOK HOUSE

SALARIYA

Published in Great Britain in MMXII by
Book House, an imprint of
The Salariya Book Company Ltd
25 Marlborough Place, Brighton BN1 1UB

1 3 5 7 9 8 6 4 2

Please visit our website at **www.salariya.com**
for **free** electronic versions of:
You Wouldn't Want to Be an Egyptian Mummy!
You Wouldn't Want to Be a Roman Gladiator!
You Wouldn't Want to Be a Polar Explorer!
**You Wouldn't Want to Sail on a 19th-Century
    Whaling Ship!**

Author: David Antram was born in Brighton,
England, in 1958. He studied at Eastbourne College
of Art and then worked in advertising for fifteen
years before becoming a full-time artist. He has
illustrated many children's non-fiction books.

Editor: Rob Walker

PB ISBN: 978-1-907184-62-8

A CIP catalogue record for this
book is available from the
British Library.

Printed and bound in China.
Printed on paper from
sustainable sources.

**WARNING: Fixatives should be
used only under adult supervision.**

Visit our websites to read interactive free web
books, stay up to date with new releases, catch
up with us on the Book House Blog, view our
electronic catalogue and more!

www.book-house.co.uk
Information books and graphic novels

www.scribobooks.com
Fiction books

www.scribblersbooks.com
Books for babies, toddlers and pre-school
children.

PAPER FROM
SUSTAINABLE
FORESTS

Follow us on Facebook and
Twitter by visiting
www.salariya.com

Contents

Making a start

Learning to draw is about looking and seeing. Keep practising and get to know your subject. Use a sketchbook to make quick drawings. Start by doodling and experimenting with shapes and patterns. There are many ways to draw; this book shows only some methods. Visit art galleries, look at artists' drawings, see how friends draw, but above all, find your own way.

Remember that practice makes perfect.
If it looks wrong, start again. Keep
working at it — the more you draw,
the more you will learn.

Materials

Try using different types of drawing paper and materials. Experiment with charcoal, wax crayons and pastels. All pens, from felt-tips to ballpoints, will make interesting marks — you could also try drawing with pen and ink on wet paper.

Silhouette is a style of drawing which mainly uses solid black shapes.

Ink silhouette

Felt-tips come in a range of line widths. The wider pens are good for filling in large areas of flat tone.

Pencil and felt-tip pen

Hard **pencils** are greyer and soft pencils are blacker. Hard pencils are graded from 6H (the hardest) through 5H, 4H, 3H and 2H to H. Soft pencils are graded from B, 2B, 3B, 4B and 5B up to 6B (the softest).

Cross hatching

Adding light and shade to a drawing with an ink pen can be tricky. Use solid ink for the very darkest areas and cross hatching (straight lines criss-crossing each other) for ordinary dark tones. Use hatching (straight lines running parallel to each other) for midtones and keep the lightest areas inkfree.

Lines drawn in **ink** cannot be erased, so keep your ink drawings sketchy and less rigid. Don't worry about mistakes as these lines can be lost in the drawing as it develops.

Hatching

Drawing tools

Here are just a few of the many tools that you can use for drawing. Let your imagination go, and have fun experimenting with all the different marks you can make.

Pencil

Watercolour pencil

Charcoal pencil

Charcoal stick

Pastels

Finger painting

Black, grey and white pastel on grey sugar paper

Each grade of **pencil** makes a different mark, from fine, grey lines through to soft, black ones. Hard pencils are graded as H, 2H, 3H, 4H, 5H and 6H (the hardest). An HB pencil is ideal for general sketching. Soft pencils are graded from B, 2B, 3B, 4B, 5B to 6B (the softest and blackest).

Watercolour pencils come in many different colours and make a line similar to an HB pencil. But paint over your finished drawing with clean water, and the lines will soften and run.

It is less messy and easier to achieve a fine line with a **charcoal pencil** than a stick of charcoal. Create soft tones by smudging lines with your finger. **Ask an adult** to spray the drawing with fixative to prevent further smudging.

Pastels are brittle sticks of powdered colour. They blend and smudge easily and are ideal for quick sketches. Pastel drawings work well on textured, coloured paper. **Ask an adult** to spray your finished drawing with fixative.

Experiment with **finger painting**. Your fingerprints make exciting patterns and textures. Use your fingers to smudge soft pencil, charcoal and pastel lines.

8

Ballpoint pens are very useful for sketching and making notes. Make different tones by building up layers of shading.

A **mapping pen** has to be dipped into bottled ink to fill the nib. Different nib shapes make different marks. Try putting a diluted ink wash over parts of the finished drawing.

Draughtsmen's pens and specialist **art pens** can produce extremely fine lines and are ideal for creating surface texture. A variety of pen nibs are available which produce different widths of line.

Felt-tip pens are ideal for quick sketches. If the ink is not waterproof, try drawing on wet paper and see what happens.

Broad-nibbed **marker pens** make interesting lines and are good for large, bold sketches. Try using a black pen for the main sketch and a grey one to block in areas of shadow.

Paintbrushes are shaped differently to make different marks. Japanese brushes are soft and produce beautiful flowing lines. Large sable brushes are good for painting a wash over a line drawing. Fine brushes are good for drawing delicate lines.

Ballpoint pen

Mapping pen

Draughtsman's pen

Felt-tip pen

Marker pen

Paintbrush

9

Perspective

If you look at any object from different viewpoints, you will see that the part that is closest to you looks larger, and the part furthest away from you looks smaller. Drawing in perspective is a way of creating a feeling of depth — of showing three dimensions on a flat surface.

The vanishing point (V.P.) is the place in a perspective drawing where parallel lines appear to meet. The position of the vanishing point depends on the viewer's eye level. Sometimes a low viewpoint can give your drawing added drama.

V.P.

V.P.

10

Two-point perspective drawing

Two-point perspective uses two
vanishing points: one for lines running
along the length of the object,
and one on the opposite side
for lines running across
the width of the
object. This gives a
very realistic
three-dimensional effect.

Low eye level
(view from below)

V.P.

V.P.

V.P.

Normal eye level.

V.P.

V.P.

High eye level
(view from above)

V.P. — vanishing point

Fairy Fashion

Fairies adore dressing up and are always looking for beautiful accessories to complement their outfits. Fairy fashions are seasonal and as autumn approaches, fairies use fallen acorn cups and conker shells to make stylish hats. Their summer collection includes fabulous flower sunhats and delightful daisy caps.

Conker

Acorn cup

Conker shell

Acorns

Conker shells and acorn cups make simple hat designs for fairies.

12

Flowers and leaves are a great starting point to create fairy hats from.

Sketching plants

Remember to take your sketchbook with you when you visit parks or woods. Study the plants and make sketches to get inspiration for your fairy fashions!

Let your imagination go. Study the distinctive shapes of petals and flower heads before you draw the fairies wearing them.

Adventurous fairies

Fairies are shy and secretive, rarely revealing themselves to humans. However, if you are lucky, one of the more adventurous ones may let you hold her on your hand.

Draw an oval shape for the fairy's head.

Head

Mark the centre of the head with two lines.

Body

Draw ovals for the body and hips.

Hips

Add lines for the arms and legs with dots for the joints. Draw in lines for the spine, shoulders and hips.

Roughly sketch the shape of your hand.

Sketch in the position of the facial features.

Join the body and the hips, to get the shape of the body.

Draw in the arms and legs using simple tube shapes.

Draw triangular shapes for the feet.

Draw in the shape of the thumb and the wrist.

Draw in the fingers using simple tube shapes.

Add the finger joints.

14

Use simple lines to position the head, hat, hair, nose, eyes and ear.

Sketch in the wings. Try to keep them symmetrical.

Add the tunic, skirt and belt.

Finish drawing the hand.

Shade areas of the head and clothes where light wouldn't reach.

Use shading for the wing pattern.

Add details to the feet and legs, adding knees and toes.

Finish the hand by drawing creases on the palm and fingers. Add a thumb nail.

Shading the hand makes it look rounded.

Using an eraser, remove any unwanted construction lines that remain.

15

Naughty Fairies

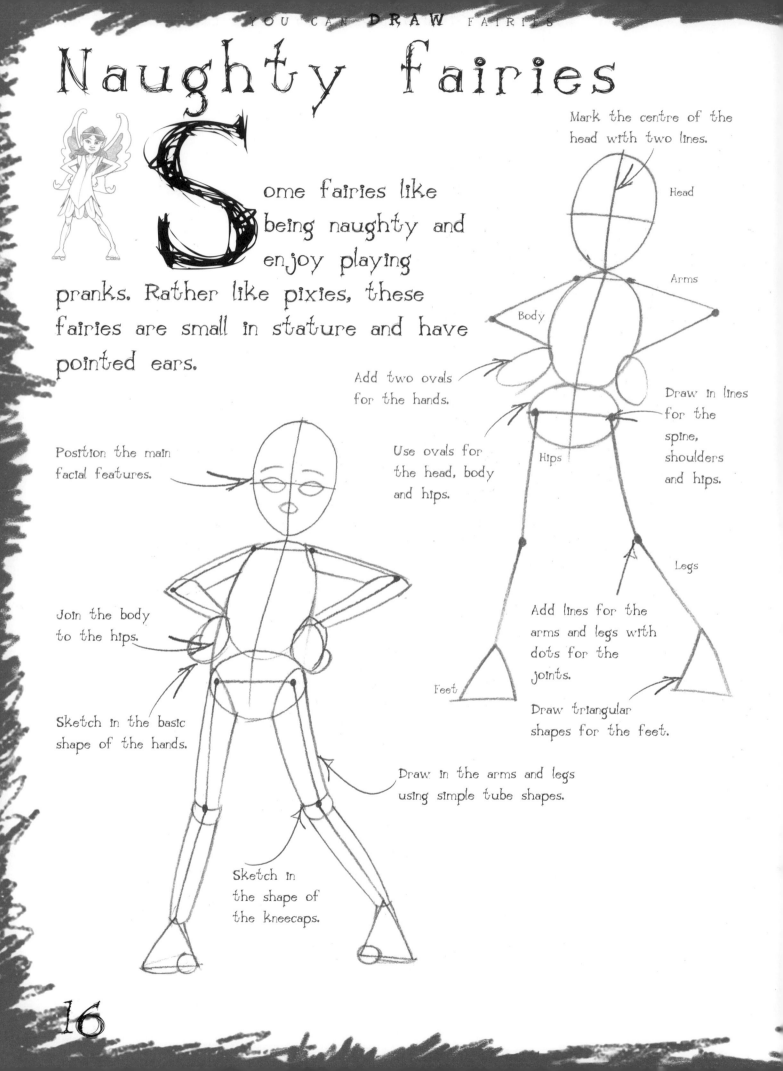

Some fairies like being naughty and enjoy playing pranks. Rather like pixies, these fairies are small in stature and have pointed ears.

Mark the centre of the head with two lines.

Head

Arms

Body

Draw in lines for the spine, shoulders and hips.

Add two ovals for the hands.

Use ovals for the head, body and hips.

Hips

Position the main facial features.

Join the body to the hips.

Sketch in the basic shape of the hands.

Legs

Add lines for the arms and legs with dots for the joints.

Feet

Draw triangular shapes for the feet.

Draw in the arms and legs using simple tube shapes.

Sketch in the shape of the kneecaps.

Sketch in the wings so they follow the line of the figure.

Add more detail to the face and sketch in the neck and pointed ears.

Draw in the hair and the outline of the clothes.

Add more detail to the hair and finish the face.

Curl the wings at their base for a three-dimensional effect.

Shading the wing pattern makes the fairy shape stand out.

Finish drawing the knees and ankles. and add the toes.

Draw veins on the petals that form the skirt.

Finish drawing the toes. Add toe nails.

Negative space
Look at the shapes left between the lines of your drawing; this can help you spot mistakes.

Shade areas like this where light wouldn't reach.

Remove any unwanted construction lines.

17

Punk fairies

Fashion–conscious fairies like seeing what humans wear and often adapt a particular style to suit themselves. Many young fairies have been spotted in punk outfits, with their colourfully dyed, spiky hair.

Mark the centre of the head with two lines.

Draw in lines for the spine, shoulders and hips.

Draw oval shapes for the head, body and hips.

Hands

Add lines for the arms and legs with dots for the joints.

Hips

Add ovals for the hands.

Draw simple shapes for the hands and feet.

Feet

Use the construction lines to place the eyes, nose, mouth and ears.

Sketch in the shapes of the fingers and thumbs.

All the weight is supported on the right leg.

Light sources

Changing the direction of the light source in a drawing can create drama and mood.

Add two lines for the wand.

Draw in the arms and legs using tube shapes. Use the dots to position the knees, ankles and elbows.

18

Add the wings.

Draw in the spiky hair and the pointed hairline.

Draw the neck and shoulders.

Sketch in the neck and sleeves of the tunic, curving them around the body.

Finish drawing the hands and fingers.

Add shading to the hair and wing patterns.

Sketch in the curved waistline and the hemline of the skirt.

Draw a star for the wand.

Sketch in the large, chunky boots.

Using the construction lines, draw a zig-zag edging on the sleeves and neckline.

Give the skirt a zig-zag hemline and draw lines up to the waist. Shade alternate panels where the light wouldn't reach.

Draw in the stripes around the arms and legs, and shade alternate stripes.

Remove any unwanted construction lines with an eraser.

Draw in the boot detail and shade them in.

19

Musical Fairies

Most fairies love to play music, the fairy flute being their favourite instrument. Throughout history, fairies have used music as a means of enchanting both animals and humans.

Draw two curved lines and a row of ovals for the shape of the flower wreath.

Add hair and place the neck and facial features.

Sketch in the hands around the flute.

Draw in the arms and legs using simple tube shapes.

Flower wreath

Flute

Draw in the flute.

Add a line for the flute.

Mark the centre of the head with two lines.

Draw in ovals for the head, body, hips and hands.

Draw in lines for the spine, shoulders and hips.

Add lines for the arms and legs with dots for the joints.

Draw triangular shapes for the feet.

Draw in the position of the big toe.

20

Draw two wings, making sure they are the same shape on either side.

Add petals to the wreath.

Add more detail to the face and hair.

Draw the flute shape.

Draw in the hands and fingers.

Add leaves and more detail to the flower wreath.

Finish the face and hair.

Start sketching in clothes, using simple shapes.

Sketch in the ankles and toes.

To finish the wings, draw in shapes like the veins of a butterfly's wings.

Add fold lines in the dress material.

Shade the backs of both hands.

Add shading to areas like this where light wouldn't reach.

Finish drawing the feet. Add toe nails and ankles.

Remove any unwanted construction lines with an eraser.

21

Fairy friends

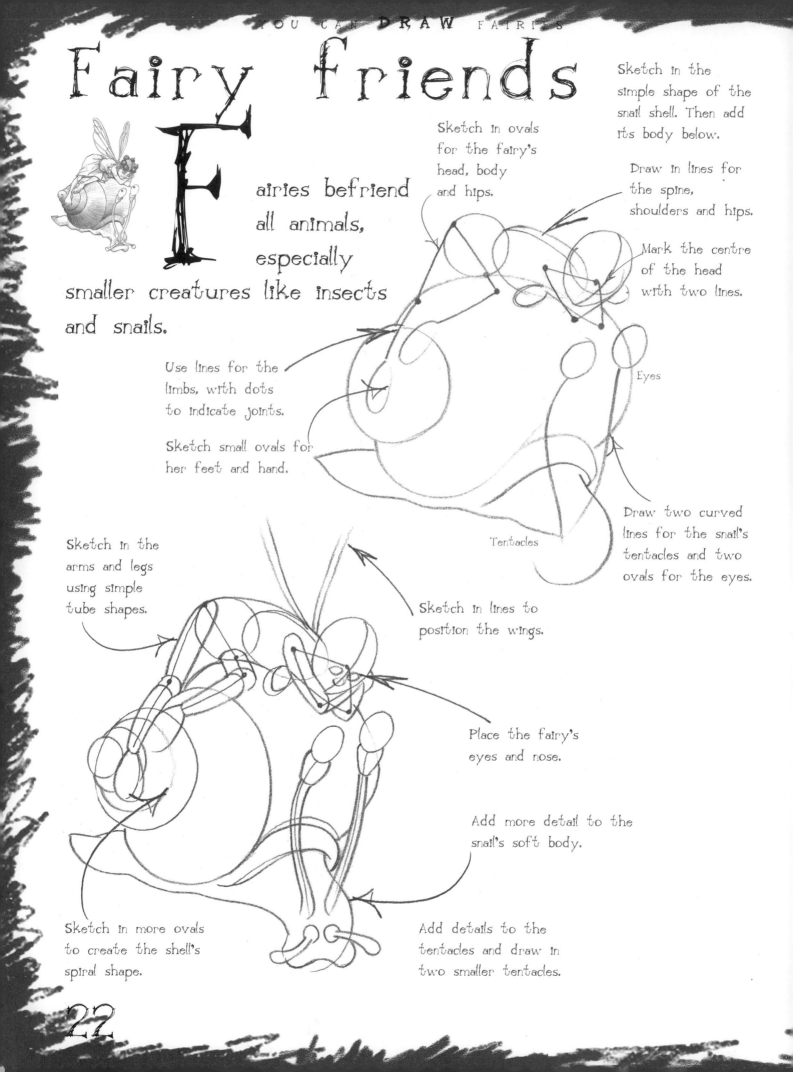

Fairies befriend all animals, especially smaller creatures like insects and snails.

Sketch in ovals for the fairy's head, body and hips.

Use lines for the limbs, with dots to indicate joints.

Sketch small ovals for her feet and hand.

Sketch in the simple shape of the snail shell. Then add its body below.

Draw in lines for the spine, shoulders and hips.

Mark the centre of the head with two lines.

Eyes

Tentacles

Draw two curved lines for the snail's tentacles and two ovals for the eyes.

Sketch in the arms and legs using simple tube shapes.

Sketch in lines to position the wings.

Place the fairy's eyes and nose.

Add more detail to the snail's soft body.

Sketch in more ovals to create the shell's spiral shape.

Add details to the tentacles and draw in two smaller tentacles.

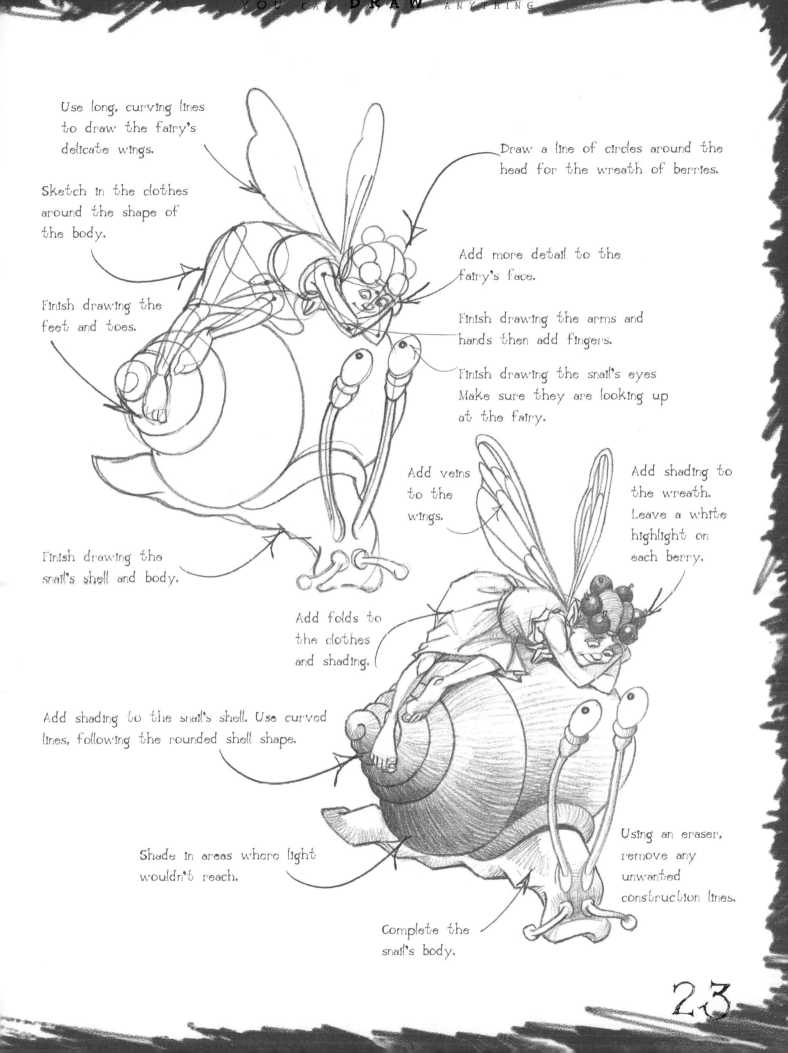

Use long, curving lines to draw the fairy's delicate wings.

Sketch in the clothes around the shape of the body.

Finish drawing the feet and toes.

Draw a line of circles around the head for the wreath of berries.

Add more detail to the fairy's face.

Finish drawing the arms and hands then add fingers.

Finish drawing the snail's eyes Make sure they are looking up at the fairy.

Add veins to the wings.

Add shading to the wreath. Leave a white highlight on each berry.

Finish drawing the snail's shell and body.

Add folds to the clothes and shading.

Add shading to the snail's shell. Use curved lines, following the rounded shell shape.

Shade in areas where light wouldn't reach.

Using an eraser, remove any unwanted construction lines.

Complete the snail's body.

23

Fairy toadstools

Not all fairies are clever, some simply have their heads in the clouds. Nevertheless these fairies do the important task of caring for magic toadstools and maintaining fairy rings.

Draw ovals for the head, body and hips.

Mark the centre of the head with two lines.

Add lines for the arms and legs, with dots for the joints.

Head

Draw lines for the spine, shoulders and hips.

Body

Hips

Draw a curved line for the flower hat.

Flower hat

Cap

Add the nose, ears, mouth and neck.

Sketch in simple shapes for the hands and feet.

Sketch in the hands, adding a thumb and finger.

Stalk

Draw a line for the stalk.

Draw the basic shape of the toadstool's cap.

Draw in the arms and legs using simple tube shapes.

Sketch a curved line to show the inside of the toadstool cap.

Draw another curved line for the stalk and an oval at the base.

24

Add a curved brim and stalk to the hat.

Stalk

Brim

Add detail to the nose, and make the chin pointed.

Add fingers and nails to the hands.

Draw in the wings pointing downwards behind him.

Draw the fairy's clothes and 3/4 length trousers.

Use lines to give shade and texture to the flower hat.

Sketch in ovals for the toadstool spots.

Toadstool

Finish the face and ears and shade under the chin.

Add veins to the wings.

Add pixie boots with long, pointed toes.

Draw in details of the clothing with its ragged edges.

Put shading under the fairy, leaving the oval spots white.

Use an eraser to remove any unwanted construction lines.

Shade areas like this where light wouldn't reach.

25

Flying fairies

Surprisingly, not all fairies are born with wings. Some fairies have their wings made from silken, spun gossamer, decorated with soft, downy feathers.

Look carefully at the angle and shape of the flying fairy before you start sketching her in.

Draw ovals for the head, body and hips.

Mark the centre of the head with two lines.

Draw in lines for the spine, shoulders and hips. Use these as a guide to position the arms and legs, adding dots for the joints.

Draw ovals for the hands and feet.

Use long curved lines to show the direction of the wings.

Wings

Place the facial features.

Draw in the arms and legs using simple tube shapes.

Draw in the shape of the hands and fingers.

Join the body to the hips with two curved lines.

Using more curved lines, draw the wings.

Sketch in the fairy's hat made of leaves and her spiky hair.

Add the shape of the ankle and draw in pointed pixie boots.

Add detail and shape to the face.

Add a bracelet.

Sketch in leaves as clothing.

Complete the wings, adding veins, a pattern and shading.

Add a zig-zag edge to the leaf skirt and draw veins on it.

Add a belt.

Finish the face. Add shading to the eyes and a shadow under the hat to make her eyes stand out.

Finish the legs and boots.

Add shading to the hands.

Remove any unwanted construction lines using an eraser.

27

Fairy Godmother

Rarely seen, Fairy Godmothers have very special, magical powers. Most children have a Fairy Godmother who has the power to help them, but alas, only once!

Mark the centre of the head with two lines.

Sketch in the hands and feet using simple shapes.

Head

Draw in lines for the spine, shoulder and hips.

Body

Draw in ovals for the head, body and shoulders.

Hips

Place the facial features and the neck.

Add lines for the arms and legs, with dots for the joints.

Add more detail to the hands, adding thumbs and fingers.

Draw in the arms and legs using simple tube shapes.

Sketch in the big toe.

28

Sketch in sharp, spiky wings.

Use long curved lines for the hair, then add a crown.

Crown

Add more detail to the facial features and draw in the shape of the face.

Add a bracelet.

Sketch in the clothes, giving shape to the bodice and waist.

Add shading to the hair and above the eyes. Use darker shading where the light wouldn't reach.

Finish off the fingers and hand shapes.

Add fold lines to the base of the skirt to show excess material.

Add veins and a pattern to the wings. Add shading to the edge of the wings.

Add detail to the bracelet and crown and draw in beads around her dress.

Add shading to areas of the bodice and skirt where light wouldn't reach.

Remove any unwanted construction lines using an eraser.

29

Woodland Fairies

Although the most numerous, woodland fairies are difficult to spot. Their ability to vanish into the undergrowth is legendary.

Look carefully at the angles and shape of this kneeling fairy.

Head

Mark the centre of the head with two lines.

Body

Draw in lines for the spine, shoulders and hips. Use these as a guide to position the ovals for the head, body and hips.

Hips

Add lines for the arms and legs with dots for joints (the head is positioned directly above the arms).

Feet

Hands

Carefully sketch in the shape and direction of the feet and hands.

Add the facial features.

Draw in the arms and legs using simple tube shapes.

Join the body to the hips.

Add thumbs to the hands.

Add detail to the face and draw in the fringe.

Using long curved lines, draw in the leaf cap.

Draw in the dress made of leaves. Add a belt around the waist.

Sketch in the shape of the foot and ankle and add toes.

Draw in the fingers and thumbs.

Complete the details of the hat and add shade to the inside.

Finish drawing the face, add shading above the eyes and to the lips.

Draw more shape into the shoulders and arms.

Add shade to these areas to show that the fairy is leaning forward.

Add zig-zag edges and veins to the leaf dress.

Finish drawing the hands and fingers.

Use an eraser to remove any unwanted construction lines.

31

Glossary

Chiaroscuro The practice of drawing high contrast pictures with a lot of black and white, but not much grey.

Composition The arrangement of the parts of a picture on the drawing paper.

Construction lines Guidelines used in the early stages of a drawing. They are usually erased later.

Fixative A type of resin used to spray over a finished drawing to prevent smudging. **It should only be used by an adult.**

Light source The direction from which the light seems to come in a drawing.

Negative space The blank space surrounding a drawing.

Perspective A method of drawing in which near objects are shown larger than faraway objects to give an impression of depth.

Proportion The correct relationship of scale between each part of the drawing.

Silhouette A drawing that shows only a flat dark shape, like a shadow.

Symmetrical The same shape on both sides.

Vanishing point The place in a perspective drawing where parallel lines appear to meet.

Index